It's Praying Time!

&

HUMILITY IS REQUIRED!

Inspired By: God the Father

Written By: Dr. Kimberly K. Clayton

It's Praying Time! & Humility Is Required!

ISBN 9780578939575

Self-Published Amazon KDP: Dr. Kimberly K. Clayton

itsprayingtime2020@gmail.com

Scriptures are noted from the following versions:

KJV – King James Version

NKJV – New King James Version

NLT – New Living Translation

AMP – Amplified

AMPC – Amplified Classic

GNT – Good News Translation

Printed in the United States of America

Dr. Kimberly K. Clayton's Books:

1) *It's Praying Time – What You Need to Know About Prayer Intercession*

2) *It's Praying Time & Soul Winning Time*

3) *It's Praying Time & No More Idols*

4) *It's Praying Time & Obedience Is Required*

Dedication

I like to dedicate this book to my late mother, Mrs. Millicent Jones who was humble and made sure to show me an example of humility. You made sure me and my siblings knew we weren't better than anyone else and no one was better than us. You believed firmly that the only time you look down on someone is when you are helping them stand back up!

Also to my daughter, Elise who even at a young age has shown a heart for the least of these. I was amazed at how you did not want anyone being mistreated. You spoke truthfully and boldly when you saw a man asking for money, "Some people don't care about that man." Your words pierced my heart and were reminder to help someone in need.

I also dedicate this book to my Grandmothers, Willene, Gracie and my bonus Grandmother (Great Aunt) Mary 😉. I have been extremely blessed to have praying Grandmothers like you, that pray and intercede for me and love me the way that you do!

Acknowledgments

I would like to acknowledge God the Father, God the Son (Jesus Christ) and The Holy Spirit for their unconditional love and patience with me. I am forever grateful for all that God has done for me. Thank you for bringing the right people at the right time into my life. God I see you working in my life and I thank you for never giving up on me.

I am thankful for my earthly Dad, Mr. Jones who would encourage me not to give up and to keep going even when I was hard hit by circumstances in life.

To those of you who are apart of "It's Praying Time", I thank you for your faithfulness to pray with me, and for me and Elise. You too have become a part of our spiritual journey and I honor you for that.

Lastly to every Humble Servant of God dedicated to do the work of the Lord without a lot of recognition, without fail, without excuses and with a spirit of excellence! I want to acknowledge you that I see you and I am so thankful for your humble example. Thank you for demonstrating humility in a loving and compassionate way. May you be encouraged and strengthened for the journey ahead, and know that I applaud you and stand in the gap for you!

Table of Contents

Introduction

Have you noticed how much pride is rampant in the world today? There is no shortage of narcissism, ego-maniacs, etc. In fact when you see leaders in particular who are wealthy, powerful and humble it is indeed rare and a breath of fresh air. Is it possible that we don't see pride and arrogance as the sin that they really are.

As time is running out we have to make the necessary adjustments quickly! God and pride do not mix together at all. In these last and evil days we have to be careful that we do not give pride and arrogance any room in any area of our lives.

The expression, "What goes up, must come down." is very true and real when it comes to pride. Have you seen where someone was very boisterous and consistently bragging about his or her accomplishments and never gave God any GLORY for what he had done in their life? Did you notice that when the person finally crossed a line and refused to humble themselves, that suddenly they were no longer on the mountaintop, but down in the valley? That is no coincidence. God's word is true, he will resist the proud.

A question I will ask you throughout this book is, "Do you want God to humble you or do you choose to humble yourself?"

We want to make the most of every opportunity to win souls for Jesus Christ. The truth is eternity is closer for some than others. We are not just living for this life, but we are surely living for the life to come. Let me encourage you do not delay in saying this Salvation Prayer. Please repeat this prayer from a sincere heart.

Dear Lord Jesus, I know that I am a sinner, and I ask you for your forgiveness. I believe you died for my sins and rose from the dead. I turn from my sins, and invite You to come into my heart and life. I ask for the Holy Spirit to dwell in me, to guide me, and to teach me all things. I choose to trust and follow You as the Son of God and LORD and Savior in Jesus name Amen and Amen.

If you repeated that prayer with a true sincerity you JUST GOT SAVED!!! We encourage you to read your Bible on a daily basis. You can download the Bible App at https://www.youversion.com/the-bible-app/. It will bless you greatly to be able to take the Bible with you everywhere you go. It even allows you to download offline versions of the Bible so you can still read the Bible without Internet access. This Bible App even reads the Bible to you, has devotionals, Bible study plans, prayers and more. Please get a paper Parallel Study Bible that has King James Version(KJV) and New Living Translation(NLT), or another version of your choice that helps you to understand the scriptures.

We are praying with you because getting saved is just the first step. Reading the Bible every day is the second step and the third step is to pray and ask God the Father to lead you to a church home where you will be planted, rooted and established in the Word of God. A good church home that teaches and preaches the Bible without watering it down. Many churches are still working for the Lord even if the doors of the church building are not physically open yet.

Lastly if you repeated the Salvation Prayer and got saved please email us at itsprayingtime2020@gmail.com, we would like to pray for you and encourage you along your spiritual journey. You can also email us your prayer requests and we would be glad to stand in the gap for you.

Chapter 1
What Is Humility?

The online Oxford Dictionaries define humility as a modest or low view of one's own importance. In other words the person is not concerned about bringing attention to oneself, but more concerned about holding someone else in high esteem.

Humility is:

- Pointing people to Jesus Christ the Son of God and God the Father
- Choosing to surrender one's life to Jesus Christ, God the Father and the Holy Spirit
- Esteeming others higher than oneself, building them up
- Honoring the Holy Spirit within us, Glorifying God
- Doing what is asked of us without murmuring, complaining or backbiting
- Encouraging others to keep going and not to give up
- Being faithful even when others are not
- Respecting authority, especially Godly authority
- God confidence, a true reliance and confidence in God the Father
- Reassurance of Salvation through Jesus Christ

- Accepting correction without becoming defensive

Humility is not:

- Bragging about oneself, accomplishments, excessive confidence in oneself
- Looking down on the poor
- Comparing oneself to others, Petty or immature competition
- Diminishing others and their self worth, so one can appear to shine “brighter”
- Thinking way too much or too highly of oneself
- False rumors, lies or slandering others
- Challenging leadership on every instruction, delegated assignments or tasks
- Refusing to submit and respect leadership, especially Godly leadership
- Consistently pointing out others and leaderships faults and mistakes with no encouragement
- Everyone else is always wrong
- Easily offended or irritated, Argumentative or defensive
- Chaotic, or full of confusion
- Murmuring, complaining, backbiting or gossiping
- Being a doormat or allowing others to consistently misuse and abuse you

Humility is the direct opposite of pride. Like the title of the book, *Humility is Required* we have to know in this hour that humility is not optional. Like the saints of old would say, "The way up in the Kingdom of God is down." Let's explore further what this expression is really telling us. It's telling us that if you want or desire to go higher in God and the things of God that you must be willing to humble yourself. Remember pride and God don't mix at all. So, if we don't humble ourselves prepare for God to humble you through life circumstances, people and experiences.

Humility is a willingness of allowing our flesh to be crucified so God the Father can be glorified! People need to see Jesus Christ in us, not our flesh on display. The more they see Jesus Christ in us the more they will be drawn to him. Our flesh is corrupted, there is no doubt about that and another way of looking at is:

Corrupted flesh = PRIDE, Crucified flesh = HUMILITY.

We have to remember that our flesh is in direct opposition with God, his Living Word and his commandments. A corrupted flesh (prideful spirit) can only accomplish so much for God and the Kingdom of God. A crucified flesh (humble spirit) there is no limit to what can be accomplished for God and the Kingdom of God.

As we allow our flesh to be crucified it won't always be easy, but it will always be worth it. An acceptance that our flesh is corrupted and full of pride is important and necessary to help facilitate the process of crucifying our flesh to bring about Godly humility. When we are not in denial it helps us because we won't fight the humility process as hard as we would when we are in denial. Sometimes when trials, tribulations and persecutions come in our life we assume that it is an attack of the enemy, which can be true. That's why it's important to know what season we are in our lives.

Even if God allows specific trials, tribulations and persecutions we have to remember that he is using these things to continue to crucify our flesh. God is using these things to test our hearts so we can see where we really are at versus where we really need to be in him. What I like about God is even if we don't pass the test he will surely give us another chance to pass the test. My prayer is that we have the discernment and wisdom to know when we fail the test, usually the Holy Spirit will convict us and there's a guilt that usually can't be released until we confess that we know we did not handle a person or particular situation the right way. This is part of the humility process and we have to learn to pray and ask the Holy Spirit to help us pass that specific test on the next try.

Humility is being able to admit when you are wrong and without a nasty attitude or defensive tone or behavior. Leaders that I admire have a beautiful humility about themselves. It's rare if at all to see them talk to others with a nasty tone even when they are in the wrong. These leaders had such a humility that they would apologize sincerely without hesitation. They would always do their best to make things right with the other person or people. Humble leaders even would apologize and make a sincere effort to reconcile even when they were not in the wrong. Getting aggressive, defensive and combative when one is wrong is a sure sign that one has more work and growing to do in the area of humility.

Humility is esteeming God the Father and Jesus Christ higher than ourselves. When we have a healthy perspective of who we are, sinners saved by Grace in comparison to a Holy God and Savior, that should make it easier to exalt God the Father and Jesus Christ. The ultimate goal is to point people toward God the Father and Jesus Christ, we should not be pointing people to ourselves. The reality is this who we are and what we achieve really does come from God the Father and Jesus Christ.

We should never want to be in a place that people rely on us so heavily that they think to come to us first. This can be dangerous territory we can't always be there for everyone all of the time, so it's important that we are exalting God the Father and Jesus Christ that people know to go to them first! Unfortunately when this happens people expect one to be God the Father and Jesus Christ, and no one person can bare such a heavy load for too long of a time. The pressure, stress and burden from people's over reliance on a mere person can cause that individual to crack under such pressure and immense responsibility. It may even cause one to throw in the towel and not continue with the ministry assignment that God has called them to.

A Godly confidence that God is the reason that you have the life that you have. Realizing that you would not be where you are if it had not been for the goodness and mercy of God the Father. That everything you have accomplished is because God gave you the strength, health, talents and abilities to achieve those goals. Humility is fulling understanding that you are nothing apart from God the Father. That you are alive because he created you and has sustained you this far.

What does the Bible say humility is? Who does the Bible say was humble? A good place to start is Moses. Even when he had a life of prestige, wealth and honor, it bothered him to see his brother and sisters being treated so harshly under the cruelty of slavery. He could have easily looked the other way, but he didn't. Even when

God revealed his plans to Moses on how he would use him to deliver his people from Pharoah, Moses did not think it was possible for him to speak because he stuttered. Moses looked at himself as not qualified or important enough to do such a large endeavor for God the Father. The scripture shows that even God was not thrilled with Moses lowly view of himself, yet his humbleness is noted because he is the one person that was able to talk face to face with God. Exodus 33:11 KJV *And the LORD spake unto Moses face to face, as a man speaketh unto his friend. And he turned again into the camp:*

Despite Moses humble view of himself he still obeyed God in the midst of his own reservations, fears and concerns. How God used Moses is one of the most powerful and amazing miracles in the Bible. I strongly believe because Moses was so humble, God could utilize him with great miracles, signs and wonders because Moses was not trying to steal any of God's glory for himself. Moses is an example that we should study and learn so much when it comes to humility.

Chapter 1 Summary

What is Humility?

- **Humility is a proper perspective about oneself, I am nothing apart from God the Father.**

- **Humility is lifting God the Father and Jesus Christ up, and not oneself.**

- **Consistently pointing people to God the Father and Jesus Christ.**

- **Esteeming others higher than myself on a consistent basis.**

- **Corrupted FLESH = PRIDE, Crucified FLESH = HUMILITY**

- **Accepting that Humility is Required, not optional with God the Father.**

Chapter 2

Who Should Demonstrate Humility?

Who should show humility? The answer is EVERYONE. Sometimes in this life as we achieve and accomplish much we can forget some of the basics that helped us to get where we were going. Overall, most people don't make it to where they are going by not being able to listen and receive constructive criticism. Let's use for example when a person starts an entry level position with a business or company. That business usually has standards, a code of ethics, mission statement, core values and performance reviews just to name a few. These are some of the guidelines that are in place to make sure that employees know what is expected of them. How can a person expect to be promoted within that company without knowing what the expectations are? How would the person know if this company is a good fit for them if they didn't know the mission statement, core values or other standards of that company?

The standards set by the company help to provide a roadmap, however it only works when the individuals do their very best to adhere (to follow) the guidelines that are set forth by the company. An employee especially a new one would be thinking in error if he or she believes that they can do whatever they want, when they want on the job and still keep the job and even be promoted. Most jobs usually have a ninety day probation period some have even as long as one year. It's during this time that the new employee gets to demonstrate that they can do the job and also can determine if this particular company is a good fit for them. The probation period does have a two way element to it.

When an employee accepts the standards and expectations of the company and his or her supervisor, and does the work that is required of them then things should move smoothly for him or her. This employee is demonstrating humility by accepting the standards, expectations and directions; and actually doing what is required of them. At some point of time this new employee can expect to come off probation, eventually be promoted into other positions as long as they stay on this track of humility. We know the opposite to be true as well, an employee that's not listening and refusing to do what's asked of them, consistently rebelling against management will unfortunately be fired during their probation.

Let's apply this to the Kingdom of God now. Born again Christians are required to be humble. Any Christian who refuses to accept God's standards, his Holy Word (Bible), his Godly leaders, his Godly wisdom, and his Godly instructions and commandments is not showing humility, he or she is showing PRIDE. Christians we are leaders in this world rather we want to be or not. We have to put away selfish thoughts that say my life is my own to do whatever I want with it. More is required of the born again believer, God is counting on us to demonstrate the love of God to a lost, hurting and dying world. It is so much better to demonstrate the love of God through humility, rather than pride.

The scripture let's Christians know that we are working unto the Lord, not mere man. Colossians 3:23-24 KJV, "And whatsoever ye do, do it heartily, as to the Lord, and not unto men; Knowing that of the Lord ye shall receive the reward of the inheritance: for ye serve the Lord Christ." It's important to see this more clearly that Jesus Christ and God the Father are our Commanders in Chief, Our Bosses, Our Top Leaders and we work for them. If a believer hasn't made this our main focal point in life, then life can be a lot more challenging than it has to be. God is looking for believers who will still do a great job even when they are mistreated, undervalued, underpaid, overworked and overlooked for the promotion. Can God count on you to shine and demonstrate humility even in the toughest of work situations?

God is not calling us to be totally misused and abused by others, even on the job. Yet, if this is the test that you have not passed you will continue to face the same and similar situations on the job until you pass. If we refuse to humble ourselves on a consistent basis, God will have to allow additional trials and tribulations to come to get our attention immediately. God desires to use us to do great works for him, but if we refuse to humble ourselves God can only utilize us up to a point. Is it possible we have been waiting on God to do something for us, while all the way God has been waiting on us to humble ourselves?

Do you want God to humble you or do you choose to humble yourself? This is a personal question that one must answer for his or herself. If you are at the place where God has to humble you, please be advised that it may mean going through great adversities, trials and tribulations. As we grow in our walk with God we want to be able to say with a sincere heart that we choose to humble ourselves. That we fully grasp that James 4:6 KJV, *"But he giveth more grace. Wherefore he saith, God resisteth the proud, but giveth grace unto the humble."* is real and should be a scripture committed not only to memory but to our hearts.

James 4:6 NLT *And he gives grace generously. As the Scripture say, "God opposes the proud, but gives grace to the humble."*

People of God we don't want God resisting and opposing us, we all know that's a fight that we cannot win. We have to humble ourselves and the sooner the better. Part of walking uprightly before God is walking in humility. As God begins to utilize us for his glory, can he trust us to handle success, achievements, power, status, authority with a gracious humility? Or we will be like so many others who have abused their authority and caused more problems than the good they originally set out to do?

As the hour grows darker we don't have time to go backwards in God. Humility is really a foundational piece of our faith. As we grow in God our humility should shine forth more and more each day. However, if the higher we go in God the more prideful we become we can be rest assured that we won't be able to stay at that level if we continue to puff up with pride. We all know the saying that refers to pride: What goes up, must come down! Even if it seems like it's been a long time coming we should never take God's longsuffering with us, as an excuse to be prideful with him and with others.

Life can become so busy at times that we can't always see where we are missing the mark. That's why it's good to slow down from time to time to reflect on one's life:

What's going well and what hasn't been going well?

Has the Holy Spirit convicted me, if so why?

Is it hard for me to admit fault?

Do people seem to oppose me often?

Do I struggle to respect leadership, especially Godly leadership?

Do I have a habit of looking down on people?

Do I have a habit of being quick to criticize people?

Do I want more mercy for myself than I extend to others?

Do I demand respect, but refuse to give others the respect they deserve?

Do I think the title I carry puts me above others?

Do I believe that others should be held to a higher standard than myself?

Is it easy or hard to forgive others? Have I been called out about my grudges and/or unforgiveness?

When in a disagreement, am I known to get the final word or say no matter what?

Is it hard for me to see other's perspectives? I believe I am always right no matter what?

When I'm right do I talk to people with respect and dignity? Do I have to raise my voice or shout to get my point across?

Do I feel because I am right, I can talk to people in any tone or any manner I wish?

Is it easier for me to see others flaws and not my own?

So, everyone is called to be humble especially in the Body of Christ. We have an obligation to God to show this lost and dying world how one should really conduct him or herself. A true leader is called to lead from the front, not the back. Those that are in the five-fold ministry should be advised that a Godly example of humility must shine forth even more so. The world has had so many examples of prideful leadership that it is critical in this late hour that God's leaders conduct themselves in a Godly humility that can't be denied or ignored.

As God utilizes the five-fold ministry the scripture as much is given, much is required should constantly be in the back of our minds. As God elevates us remember that (elevation, exaltation, promotion) all comes from God the Father, not ourselves. Psalm 75:6-7 KJV *For promotion cometh neither from the east, nor from the west, nor from the south. But God is the judge: he putteth down one, and setteth up another.* As God does great things for us whether we are the Apostle, Prophet, Evangelist, Pastor or Teacher we should have a consistent discipline in giving God the glory for all he is doing in us and through us. Five-fold ministry leaders it is extremely important that as God utilizes us for his glory that even when people are drawn to you and sing your praises, that is a good time to consistently say out of one's mouth, "To God be the Glory!" Not only should we say it from our mouths, but we should say it from sincere hearts.

It is a blessing for people to be drawn to us and for them to encourage us, and yes sometimes it means that people serve us, but we are still required to be a servant and demonstrate consistent humility. We know truly that it is a honor and a privilege to be chosen by God the Father, that he did not have to choose us and he can raise up and qualify others when we refuse to humble ourselves. A

Godly Apostle, Prophet, Evangelist, Pastor or Teacher really has the deeper understanding that we do not want to imitate this world and have our flesh on display, that we must have Jesus on display at all times. Those that are in our ministries need to see a Godly humility shown to them in our actions, decisions, conversations, works, interactions so they know that God's hand is on our lives and what's expected of them as well.

When a leader, especially a Godly leader is not humble those who are following or being led usually see it right away. Even if they don't call the leader out on it at that time, when we do or say something that lacks humility they have witnessed it and sometimes we may never know the full impact of what it does to our followers. Yet, being prideful unfortunately can cause serious problems and even distractions to those who are watching us, let's remember that even unbelievers are watching us too.

People talk one way or another, but we don't want to give them ammunition to use against us. We don't want people distracted, talking about how arrogant, or prideful we are now that God has blessed us with this or allowed us to accomplish great works for him. The more focused we are on conducting ourselves in humility the better. We have no control over people's thoughts or conversations about us, but we do have control over the way we conduct ourselves on a daily basis both publicly and privately. We would rather any talks of pride or arrogance would be found not to be the truth about us.

It's important that we turn our focus to the humble leader Moses. Numbers 12:3 KJV *(Now the man Moses was very meek, above all the men which were upon the face of the earth.)* Dictionary.com defines meek as quiet, gentle, and easily imposed on; submissive and is a synonym for humble. As I have studied the scriptures it stands out to me that each patriarch or matriarch of the faith is usually known for a strength in at least one area. Oh what a blessing it was for Moses to be remembered and noted for his humility. The scriptures are here to help guide us and encourage us for the journey we have to walk through in this life. Also, a reminder what we will be remembered for when we are no longer here?

All believers are required to be humble, but it is even more so for those who are within the five-fold ministry that we are studying Moses's example of humility in his life, decisions, actions, long-suffering with the people and his walk with God. A personal question that we all need to ask ourselves is this, "Do I struggle with humility?" If the answer is yes or no, we all need to study the scriptures on Moses example of humility. Yet, if this is an area of struggle it is a good idea to study scriptures on humility and pride. We always want to know what God says concerning a topic, and put those scriptures to memorization, meditation and application in our lives. God's word purifies us and helps us to know what to do and how to handle situations better.

Moses demonstrated humility long before he was used for God's greatness to deliver God's people in a most miraculous fashion. Although Moses was raised in a life of luxury and royalty he was not content with that as he saw his people's suffering.

Hebrews 11:24-25 KJV *By faith Moses, when he was come to years, refused to be called the son of Pharaoh's daughter; Choosing rather to suffer affliction with the people of God, than to enjoy the pleasures of sin for a season;*

Exodus 2:11-12 KJV *And it came to pass in those days, when Moses was grown, that he went out unto his brethren, and looked on their burdens: and he spied an Egyptian smiting an Hebrew, one of his brethren. And he looked this way and that way, and when he saw that there was no man, he slew the Egyptian, and hid him in the sand.*

Exodus 2:16-17 KJV *Now the priest of Midian had seven daughters: and they came and drew water, and filled the troughs to water their father's flock. And the shepherds came and drove them away: but Moses stood up and helped them, and watered their flock.*

Exodus 3:1 KJV *Now Moses kept the flock of Jethro his father in law, the priest of Midian: and he led the flock to the backside of the desert, and came to the mountain of God, even to Horeb.*

The scriptures above show that Moses was consistent in his humility. Moses had a deeper sense of justice within him and was not shy about standing up for those who could not defend themselves. Moses was bothered when he saw the Egyptian beating a fellow Hebrew and Moses was yet again bothered to see the shepherds try to bully Midian's seven daughters. Moses may not have known at those times, but God put a strong advocacy within him that he would be the deliverer that God was calling him to be for the people of Israel. Also, Moses was a shepherd for his father in law, the scriptures lets us see that those who were shepherds were usually humble. The occupation of shepherd especially in Biblical Times was usually considered a lowly position, not uncommon to hire others to tend to the flock.

In today's vernacular we can easily see or say that Moses literally went from riches to rags. He was raised in the palace, given the best education, ate the best food, had the best apparel (high end clothing), and could enjoy all that royal life had to offer; yet he was not satisfied that his life was going quite well for him when his fellow

Hebrews were suffering such hardship under the cruelty and oppression of slavery.

I must say what really stood out from the scriptures about Moses was that you could see he did not see himself above or separately from his fellow Israelites. His viewpoint came from a strong background of humility, Moses did not see himself apart from his people. Even with all that he had been blessed with, he did not esteem himself higher than the Hebrews. Moses did not look down on the Hebrews but had a concern and compassion for their suffering and afflictions.

Exodus 3:2-6 KJV *And the angel of the LORD appeared unto him in a flame of fire out of the midst of a bush: and he looked, and, behold, the bush burned with fire, and the bush was not consumed. And Moses said, I will now turn aside, and see this great sight, why the bush is not burnt. And when the LORD saw that he turned aside to see, God called unto him out of the midst of the bush, and said, Moses, Moses. And he said, Here am I. And he said, Draw not nigh hither: put off thy shoes from off thy feet, for the place whereon thou standest is holy ground. Moreover he said, I am the God of thy father, the God of Abraham, the God of Isaac, and the God of Jacob. And Moses hid his face; for he was afraid to look upon God.*

What an experience this must have been for Moses, here God is speaking to him face to face through a burning bush that does not burn up! Moses shows humility again by covering his face because he was afraid to look at God.

Exodus 3:7-11 KJV *And the LORD said, I have surely seen the affliction of my people which are in Egypt, and have heard their cry by reason of their taskmasters; for I know their sorrows; And I am come down to deliver them out of the hand of the Egyptians, and to bring them up out of that land unto a good land and a large, unto a land flowing with milk and honey; unto the place of the Canaanites, and the Hittites, and the Amorites, and the Perizzites, and the Hivites, and the Jebusites. Now therefore, behold, the cry of the children of Israel is come unto me: and I have also seen the oppression wherewith the Egyptians oppress them. Come now therefore, and I will send thee unto Pharaoh, that thou mayest bring forth my people the children of Israel out of Egypt. And Moses said unto God, Who am I, that I should go unto Pharaoh, and that I should bring forth the children of Israel out of Egypt?*

Remember how Moses had a deep sense of justice and advocacy, well it's no surprise that God does too. In Exodus 3:7-11 it is clear that God has heard the cries of the Israelites and that he will deliver them through Moses. Even with Moses knowing that this is God speaking to him, Moses still responds in a such a humble way. Moses knows that he is a mere man, and cannot deliver the people of Israel in his own strength.

Let's circle back to Moses journey from riches to rags. Remember the expression, **"The way up in the Kingdom (of God) is down."** I can't help but notice throughout the Bible whenever God is going to use someone greatly for his glory a season of lowliness usually comes well before the great and extraordinary that the Lord has in mind for that individual. In this season of lowliness it is during that time that God tests that individual's heart to see if they will remain faithful to God and to the commands that he has given to him or her.

The season of lowliness can also be known as a time of consecration. The Wikihow.com in the article from October 23rd, 2019 "How to Consecrate Yourself" defines consecration as, "The act of setting yourself aside and dedicating yourself to deity, and that deity almost always refers to the God of Christianity." I'll take it a step further to say that God usually consecrates you during a season of lowliness, because the majority of the time God has to separate you from people, places, things to elevate you. God did exactly that with Moses he was truly taken out into the wilderness so God could prepare and equip him for his special assignment of delivering God's people from Pharaoh.

Let's learn from God and Moses example here. Although Moses was afraid to look at God's face, Moses was not afraid to be alone with God. We should all strive for alone time with God and not fear being in his presence.

It's in those quiet moments that we can receive our Heavenly instructions, assignments, tasks and goals from God the Father. It can be hard to hear from God the Father when we have a lot of people around us constantly day in and day out. So, if you are reading this book and find yourself in a lowly place or wilderness experience presently or in the future be encouraged that God has something great for you to do, remember to partner with God during this experience. Sometimes the wilderness experience is not easy and it can feel like people have abandoned you. Be rest assured that when God calls you to this place it's not necessarily the people abandoning you; but God calling you aside to spend more time with him so you can be prepared for the assignments and calling on your life.

Let's look at some more scriptures of Moses' humility.

Exodus 4:10-12 KJV *And Moses said unto the LORD, O my LORD, I am not eloquent, neither heretofore, nor since thou hast spoken unto thy servant: but I am slow of speech, and of a slow tongue. And the LORD said unto him, Who hath made man's mouth? or who maketh the dumb, or deaf, or the seeing, or the blind? have not I the LORD? Now therefore go, and I will be with thy mouth, and teach thee what thou shalt say.*

Exodus 4:18-20 KJV *And Moses went and returned to Jethro his father in law, and said unto him, Let me go, I pray thee, and return unto my brethren which are in Egypt, and see whether they be yet alive. And Jethro said to Moses, Go in peace. And the LORD said unto Moses in Midian, Go, return into Egypt: for all the men are dead which sought thy life. And Moses took his wife and his sons, and set them upon an ass, and he returned to the land of Egypt: and Moses took the rod of God in his hand.*

Moses was concerned about his speech but God had the power to change that for him. As humble as Moses was I'm not surprised that he did not want to speak in front of a large number of people. So we know that God allows Moses's, brother Aaron to be the mouthpiece but God gives the instructions to Moses who tells Aaron what to say. Moses was submitted to the authority over him, he seeks his father in law's blessing to go back to Egypt. Moses was a consistent display of humility. It's no wonder that God could use him to be a mighty prophet and deliverer for the children of Israel.

Moses was not power hungry. What do I mean by that? I am so glad you asked. Moses did not mind sharing the leadership role. Moses seemed quite glad to allow Aaron to speak directly to the people, in fact he pleaded with God that he send someone else. Moses knew that he needed help. One could infer that Moses was not only humbled but actually overwhelmed by what God was calling him to do.

The following scriptures show how Moses knew his own limitations and was humble enough to ask for help.

Exodus 4:13-17 NLT *But Moses again pleaded, "Lord, please! Send anyone else." Then the LORD became angry with Moses. "All right," he said. "What about your brother, Aaron the Levite? I know he speaks well. And look! He is on his way to meet you now. He will be delighted to see you. Talk to him, and put the words in his mouth. I will be with both of you as you speak, and I will instruct you both in what to do. Aaron will be your spokesman to the people. He will be your mouthpiece, and you will stand in the place of God for him, telling him what to say. And take your shepherd's staff with you, and use it to perform the miraculous signs I have shown you."*

Numbers 11:10-14 KJV *Then Moses heard the people weep throughout their families, every man in the door of his tent: and the anger of the LORD was kindled greatly; Moses also was displeased. And Moses said unto the LORD, Wherefore hast thou afflicted thy servant? and wherefore have I not found favour in thy sight, that thou layest the burden of all this people upon me? Have I conceived all this people? have I begotten them, that thou shouldest say unto me, Carry them in thy bosom, as a nursing father beareth the sucking child, unto the land which thou swarest unto their fathers? Whence should I have flesh to give unto all this people? for they weep unto me, saying,*

Give us flesh, that we may eat. I am not able to bear all this people alone, because it is too heavy for me.

Moses was even humble enough to listen his father in-law's advice on how to avoid being burned out.

Exodus 18:13-27 NLT *The next day, Moses took his seat to hear the people's disputes against each other. They waited before him from morning till evening. When Moses' father-in-law saw all that Moses was doing for the people, he asked, "What are you really accomplishing here? Why are you trying to do all this alone while everyone stands around you from morning till evening?" Moses replied, "Because the people come to me to get a ruling from God. When a dispute arises, they come to me, and I am the one who settles the case between the quarreling parties. I inform the people of God's decrees and give them his instructions." "This is not good!" Moses' father-in-law exclaimed. "You're going to wear yourself out—and the people, too. This job is too heavy a burden for you to handle all by yourself. Now listen to me, and let me give you a word of advice, and may God be with you. You should continue to be the people's representative before God, bringing their disputes to him. Teach them God's decrees, and give them his instructions. Show them how to conduct their lives. But select from all the people some capable, honest men who fear God and hate bribes. Appoint them as leaders over groups of one thousand, one hundred, fifty, and ten. They should always be available to solve the people's common disputes, but have them bring the major cases to you. Let the leaders decide the smaller matters themselves. They will help you carry the load, making the task easier for you. If you follow this advice, and if God commands you to do so, then you will be able to endure the pressures, and all these people will go home in peace." Moses listened to his father-in-law's advice and followed his suggestions. He chose capable men from all over Israel and appointed them as leaders over the people. He put them in charge of groups of one thousand, one hundred, fifty, and ten. These men were always available to solve the people's common disputes. They brought the major cases to Moses, but they took care of the smaller matters themselves. Soon after this, Moses said good-bye to his father-in-law, who returned to his own land.*

Now we will look at Joseph's humility process. As we read Genesis chapter 37 we will see that when Joseph was young he was not humble, in fact he was spoiled by his father because he was the youngest son at the time, and this wife had a hard time having children so it was a miracle that Joseph was born. Jacob loved Joseph more than his brothers and treated him better than the rest. We can see that the brothers had reasons to dislike Joseph, in fact the scriptures say they hated him.

Genesis 37:1-4 NKJV *Now Jacob dwelt in the land where his father was a stranger, in the land of Canaan.*

This is the history of Jacob. Joseph, being seventeen years old, was feeding the flock with his brothers. And the lad was with the sons of Bilhah and the sons of Zilpah, his father's wives; and Joseph brought a bad report of them to his father. Now Israel loved Joseph more than all his children, because he was the son of his old age. Also he made him a tunic of many colors. But when his brothers saw that their father loved him more than all his brothers, they hated him and could not speak peaceably to him.

We will read more about Joseph and his dreams, but I would like to give a word of caution here. Just because God reveals or shows something to you in a dream does not mean that you are supposed to share it with anyone. The most humble approach is to ask God for his permission to share the dream. But let's read the following scriptures to see Joseph's approach.

Genesis 37:5-8 NKJV *Now Joseph had a dream, and he told it to his brothers; and they hated him even more. So he said to them, "Please hear this dream which I have dreamed: There we were, binding sheaves in the field. Then behold, my sheaf arose and also stood upright; and indeed your sheaves stood all around and bowed down to my sheaf." And his brothers said to him, "Shall you indeed reign over us? Or shall you indeed have dominion over us?" So they hated him even more for his dreams and for his words.*

So, Genesis 37:8 really make a point even more clear that his brothers' hatred for him was increasing. I wonder sometimes was Joseph even aware of how they really felt about him? Was Joseph's pride blinding him to the fact that his brothers really hated him, not just for being the favorite, but for his dream and his words? Nevertheless this is something we should all be aware and that's why it is very important to be in tune with the Holy Spirit. Besides that it is known when others are not treated fairly, they tend to resent and despise those who are; and when things aren't going well for others we have to be careful about bragging about how well things are going for us. Just a few points to think about. We will read more about Joseph in the following scriptures.

Genesis 37:9-11 NKJV *Then he dreamed still another dream and told it to his brothers, and said, "Look, I have dreamed another dream. And this time, the sun, the moon, and the eleven stars bowed down to me." So he told it to his father and his brothers; and his father rebuked him and said to him, "What is this dream that you have dreamed? Shall your mother and I and your brothers indeed come to bow down to the earth before you?" And his brothers envied him, but his father kept the matter in mind.*

Again we can see from Genesis 37:9-11 that Joseph still had not learned to be quiet about his dreams. This time he upsets even Jacob, but the scriptures let us know that now his brothers have gone from hating him to envying him. Oh, it is sad that it seems that Joseph does not care about how his brothers view him, and he has so much pride he does not care about offending his own dad and mom. Let's keep reading.

Genesis 37:12-16 NKJV *Then his brothers went to feed their father's flock in Shechem. And Israel said to Joseph, "Are not your brothers feeding the flock in Shechem? Come, I will send you to them." So he said to him, "Here I am." Then he said to him, "Please go and see if it is well with your brothers and well with the flocks, and bring back word to me." So he sent him out of the Valley of Hebron, and he went to Shechem. Now a certain man found him, and there he was, wandering in the field. And the man asked him, saying, "What are you seeking?" So he said, "I am seeking my brothers. Please tell me where they are feeding their flocks."*

Again if Joseph were more in tune with his brothers this would have been a good time to warn Jacob how his brothers really felt about him. It was not a good idea to have Joseph spying on his brothers especially, after he revealed the two dreams to them and their anger and hatred was yet intensifying against him. The lack of humility on Joseph part continues to show that he doesn't know if he refuses to humble himself that God will humble him through various circumstances. Let's keep reading and learning as we go.

Genesis 37:17-20 NKJV *And the man said, "They have departed from here, for I heard them say, 'Let us go to Dothan.' " So Joseph went after his brothers and found them in Dothan. Now when they saw him afar off, even before he came near them, they conspired against him to kill him. Then they said to one another, "Look, this dreamer is coming! Come therefore, let us now kill him and cast him into some pit; and we shall say, 'Some wild beast has devoured him.' We shall see what will become of his dreams!"*

As we read those scriptures we see that Joseph's brothers have become so full of hatred that they start planning on how they could kill him. God has warned all of us about hating one another, my prayer is that if there is any hatred in your heart that you choose to release it and forgive whoever has angered you so you can live the life of love that God is calling you too. Even 1 John 3:15 NKJV *Whoever hates his brother is a murderer, and you know that no murderer has eternal life abiding in him.* The more we study God's word the better understanding we will gain, so we can guard our hearts against everything that's not like God. Even though the brothers are plotting against Joseph, it's interesting that they think they can kill his dreams too. A word of encouragement for all of us is that, what God says will come to pass, it will come to pass no matter how people fight against it, no one can stop the sovereign plans of ALMIGHTY GOD!

Genesis 37:21-36 NKJV *But Reuben heard it, and he delivered him out of their hands, and said, "Let us not kill him." And Reuben said to them, "Shed no blood, but cast him into this pit which is in the wilderness, and do not lay a hand on him"—that he might deliver him out of their hands, and bring him back to his father. So it came to pass, when Joseph had come to his brothers, that they stripped Joseph of his tunic, the tunic of many colors that was on him. Then they took him and cast him into a pit. And the pit was empty; there was no water in it. And they sat down to eat a meal. Then they lifted their eyes and looked, and there was a company of Ishmaelites, coming from Gilead with their camels, bearing spices, balm, and myrrh, on their way to carry them down to Egypt. So Judah said to his brothers, "What profit is there if we kill our brother and conceal his blood? Come and let us sell him to the Ishmaelites, and let not our hand be upon him, for he is our brother and our flesh." And his brothers listened. Then Midianite traders passed by; so the brothers pulled Joseph up and lifted him out of the pit, and sold him to the Ishmaelites for twenty shekels of silver. And they took Joseph to Egypt. Then Reuben returned to the pit, and indeed Joseph was not in the pit; and he tore his clothes. And he returned to his brothers and said, "The lad is no more; and I, where shall I go?" So they took Joseph's tunic, killed a kid of the goats, and dipped the tunic in the blood. Then they sent the tunic of many colors, and they brought it to their father and said, "We have found this. Do you know whether it is your son's tunic or not?" And he recognized it and said, "It is my son's tunic. A wild beast has devoured him. Without doubt Joseph is torn to pieces." Then Jacob tore his clothes, put sackcloth on his waist, and mourned for his son many days. And all his sons and all his daughters arose to comfort him; but he refused to be comforted, and he said, "For I shall go down into the grave to my son in mourning." Thus his father wept for him. Now the Midianites had sold him in Egypt to Potiphar, an officer of Pharaoh and captain of the guard.*

As we read the remaining scriptures we can see that Joseph was in serious trouble, but the mercy of God shows up in the oldest brother, Reuben who says they should not kill Joseph, does not want any shedding of his blood and ultimately had a plan to rescue Joseph from the pit later on and return him to Jacob. Unfortunately, Judah gets the idea to sell Joseph to slave traders, and we see Reuben is quite distraught to see that Joseph is not in the pit when he returns to rescue him. Reuben and his brothers don't know that God has a plan far greater than they could ever know about it, and that is why Joseph is allowed to be sold into slavery.

Eventually in Genesis 39 Joseph is falsely accused by Potiphar's wife and he is wrongly imprisoned. In your own time please read Genesis chapters 39-50 to see how everything turns out for Joseph and his brothers. We will do a highlights review of Joseph's journey of humility and

God's ultimate plan to save them all. Genesis 40 Joseph uses his God-given ability to interpret dreams for the King's butler and baker. Genesis 40:14-15 NKJV *But remember me when it is well with you, and please show kindness to me; make mention of me to Pharaoh, and get me out of this house. For indeed I was stolen away from the land of the Hebrews; and also I have done nothing here that they should put me into the dungeon."* From this scripture we can see that the humility process is still not done yet in Joseph, that he still is thinking of himself too much. When trouble comes that's the time to seek God like never before, and ask him whole heartedly what have I done wrong and how can I make it right? Sometimes we want to get out of situations at our own hands and abilities versus waiting until God delivers us from that trial. Genesis 44 we see that Joseph tests his brothers hearts to see if they really are sorry for what they have done to him. He plans to keep Benjamin in slavery, but Judah intervenes and says let me stay in his place. Genesis 44:33-34 NKJV *Now therefore, please let your servant remain instead of the lad as a slave to my lord, and let the lad go up with his brothers. For how shall I go up to my father if the lad is not with me, lest perhaps I see the evil that would come upon my father?"*

Genesis 45:3-8 NKJV *Then Joseph said to his brothers, "I am Joseph; does my father still live?" But his brothers could not answer him, for they were dismayed in his presence. And Joseph said to his brothers, "Please come near to me." So they came near. Then he said: "I am Joseph your brother, whom you sold into Egypt. But now, do not therefore be grieved or angry with yourselves because you sold me here; for God sent me before you to preserve life. For these two years the famine has been in the land, and there are still five years in which there will be neither plowing nor harvesting. And God sent me before you to preserve a posterity for you in the earth, and to save your lives by a great deliverance. So now it was not you who sent me here, but God; and He has made me a father to Pharaoh, and lord of all his house, and a ruler throughout all the land of Egypt.*

From these scriptures we can see that Joseph is more humble now and has forgiven his brothers. Joseph does his best to let his brothers know that he is not angry with them and does not want his brothers to be angry with themselves. The way Joseph can say that God sent him to Egypt so he could save them now is a very humble statement. Joseph is giving God the glory, and no longer glorifying himself.

Even when Jacob passes away Joseph's brothers still have guilt about how they treated Joseph. Genesis 50:15-21 NKJV *When Joseph's brothers saw that their father was dead, they said, "Perhaps Joseph will hate us, and may actually repay us for all the evil which we did to him." So they sent messengers to Joseph, saying, "Before your father died he commanded, saying, 'Thus you shall say to*

Joseph: "I beg you, please forgive the trespass of your brothers and their sin; for they did evil to you." ' Now, please, forgive the trespass of the servants of the God of your father." And Joseph wept when they spoke to him. Then his brothers also went and fell down before his face, and they said, "Behold, we are your servants." Joseph said to them, "Do not be afraid, for am I in the place of God? But as for you, you meant evil against me; but God meant it for good, in order to bring it about as it is this day, to save many people alive. Now therefore, do not be afraid; I will provide for you and your little ones." And he comforted them and spoke kindly to them. Joseph still demonstrates humility, love and compassion towards his brothers and does not take revenge on them. Joseph has truly matured and has been humbled and continues to be humble even toward his brothers who once hated him!

So we can see as we studied Moses and Joseph that both their journeys with God were quite different. Moses chose to humble himself and give up the life of royalty, riches and possessions. Whereas Joseph had to be stripped of the good life he had, endure slavery, false imprisonment, but when the time was right he was promoted to the second highest position in the land, only the King of Egypt was higher than him. Yes God had a great plan to save Joseph and his family from the famine that would come many years later, but this plan still involved humbling Joseph. Even when Joseph is brought before Pharoah to interpret the dreams, Joseph is quick to give God the credit and the glory! Genesis 41:14-16 NKJV *Then Pharaoh sent and called Joseph, and they brought him quickly out of the dungeon; and he shaved, changed his clothing, and came to Pharaoh. And Pharaoh said to Joseph, "I have had a dream, and there is no one who can interpret it. But I have heard it said of you that you can understand a dream, to interpret it." So Joseph answered Pharaoh, saying, "It is not in me; God will give Pharaoh an answer of peace."*

God's word shows us we can choose to humble ourselves or God will humble us. The scriptures keep reminding us that when it comes to GOD ALMIGHTY, HUMILITY IS REQUIRED.

Chapter 2 – Summary

Who Should Demonstrate Humility?

- EVERYONE

- Especially the five-fold ministry: Apostles, Prophets, Evangelists, Pastors, Teachers

- Humility must shine forth from Believers during this critical time

- The lowliness or wilderness season is used by God the Father to consecrate us for our great assignments.

    - God requires our attention and needs us to spend quality time with him

- God has to separate us to elevate us.

- God's word is true and consistently warns and informs us that no matter who you are either you choose to humble yourself or God will.

- Remember the way up in the Kingdom of God is down.
    - The humility process has to take place; therefore humility is required by God!

Chapter 3
Why Should We Demonstrate Humility?

Why should we demonstrate humility? Jesus Christ is the ultimate display of humility. To know that God had a plan to save humanity, and that plan involved Jesus Christ coming to this earth and dying on the cross for the world's (our) sins. Sometimes life can throw so many things at us, that we do not always take time to think about what Jesus Christ did for us on Calvary. And before we even get that far, just imagine knowing that you have several assignments to fulfill as Jesus Christ, but the ULTIMATE ASSIGNMENT IS TO DIE ON THE CROSS. The fact that Jesus Christ would be willing to die for our sins and he himself was without sin says a WHOLE LOT. In laymen terms Jesus was taking the blame for our sins, when he himself was blameless or without any blame, without any sins!

Let's be honest there are people who are to blame in different situations but refuse to take responsibility for their actions and decisions. Overall most people get upset for being blamed for things that they did not do. Let alone will not pay the consequences for something that they did not do. That type of nobility, loyalty and humility is very hard to find these days. Yet, we can still praise and thank God for Jesus being a willing sacrifice, being obedient even until death on the cross. Philippians 2:8 KJV *And being found in fashion as a man, he* ***humbled*** *himself, and became obedient unto death, even the death of the cross.*

The following scriptures are a reminder of what Jesus went through just before he was arrested in the Garden of Gethsemane.

Matthew 26:36-45 KJV *Then cometh Jesus with them unto a place called Gethsemane, and saith unto the disciples, Sit ye here, while I go and pray yonder. And he took with him Peter and the two sons of Zebedee, and began to be sorrowful and very heavy. Then saith he unto them, My soul is exceeding sorrowful, even unto death: tarry ye here, and watch with me. And he went a little farther, and fell on his face, and prayed, saying, O my Father, if it be possible, let this cup pass from me: nevertheless not as I will, but as thou wilt. And he cometh unto the disciples, and findeth them asleep, and saith unto Peter, What, could ye not watch with me one hour? Watch and pray, that ye enter not into temptation: the spirit indeed is willing, but the flesh is weak. He went away again the second time, and prayed, saying, O my Father, if this cup may not pass away from me, except I drink it, thy will be done. And he came and found them asleep again: for their eyes were heavy. And he left them, and went away again, and prayed the third time, saying the same words. Then cometh he to his disciples, and saith unto them, Sleep on now, and take your rest: behold, the hour is at hand, and the Son of man is betrayed into the hands of sinners.*

Mark 14:32-41 KJV *And they came to a place which was named Gethsemane: and he saith to his disciples, Sit ye here, while I shall pray. And he taketh with him Peter and James and John, and began to be sore amazed, and to be very heavy; And saith unto them, My soul is exceeding sorrowful unto death: tarry ye here, and watch. And he went forward a little, and fell on the ground, and prayed that, if it were possible, the hour might pass from him. And he said, Abba, Father, all things are possible unto thee; take away this cup from me: nevertheless not what I will, but what thou wilt. And he cometh, and findeth them sleeping, and saith unto Peter, Simon, sleepest thou? couldest not thou watch one hour? Watch ye and pray, lest ye enter into temptation. The spirit truly is ready, but the flesh is weak. And again he went away, and prayed, and spake the same words. And when he returned, he found them asleep again, (for their eyes were heavy,) neither wist they what to answer him. And he cometh the third time, and saith unto them, Sleep on now, and take your rest: it is enough, the hour is come; behold, the Son of man is betrayed into the hands of sinners.*

Luke 22:39-46 KJV *And he came out, and went, as he was wont, to the mount of Olives; and his disciples also followed him. And when he was at the place, he said unto them, Pray that ye enter not into temptation. And he was withdrawn from them about a stone's cast, and kneeled down, and prayed, Saying, Father, if thou be willing, remove this cup from me: nevertheless not my will, but thine, be done. And there appeared an angel unto him from heaven, strengthening him. And being in an agony he prayed more earnestly: and his sweat was as it were great drops of blood falling down to the ground. And when he rose up from prayer, and was come to his disciples, he found them sleeping for sorrow, And said unto them, Why sleep ye? rise and pray, lest ye enter into temptation.*

As I read these scriptures over the years I can't help but notice the intense agony that Jesus Christ was experiencing as his time was drawing near to be crucified on the cross. The anguish that he was going through is shown in these scriptures. Look at how he needs his inner circle of disciples to watch and pray with him, but they cannot. Think about the times when you needed people to support and help you, but they could not. That does not feel good, knowing you have been there for them in so many ways, and now when you need them they just can't come through the way you need them too.

Jesus Christ is about to face the most intense moments of his life and he has to do it alone. Yet, Jesus knew in the midst of his anguish that God the Father was there for him, but he had to pray to him. Jesus knew he could gain strength and endurance when he prayed. The Gospel of Luke tells us that an angel appeared and strengthened Jesus during his time of great sorrow, anguish and distress. When we see what Jesus went through in the Garden of Gethsemane it's a reminder that we should not take what he did for this whole world for granted.

Now mind you, Jesus endured a great deal of affliction and torture even before he was actually crucified. The way he was punched, spit on, slapped, mocked, lied on and whipped unmercifully are also reminders of what Jesus Christ had to endure so he could be crucified for the world's sins. The way Jesus Christ was whipped, he could not carry his own cross without the help of Simon. Mark 15:21 KJV *And they compel one Simon a Cyrenian, who passed by, coming out of the country, the father of Alexander and Rufus, to bear his cross.*

The following scriptures describe what Jesus went through on the cross.

Luke 23:33-47 KJV *And when they were come to the place, which is called Calvary, there they crucified him, and the malefactors, one on the right hand, and the other on the left. Then said Jesus, Father, forgive them; for they know not what they do. And they parted his raiment, and cast lots. And the people stood beholding. And the rulers also with them derided him, saying, He saved others; let him save himself, if he be Christ, the chosen of God. And the soldiers also mocked him, coming to him, and offering him vinegar, And saying, If thou be the king of the Jews, save thyself. And a superscription also was written over him in letters of Greek, and Latin, and Hebrew, THIS IS THE KING OF THE JEWS. And one of the malefactors which were hanged railed on him, saying, If thou be Christ, save thyself and us. But the other answering rebuked him, saying, Dost not thou fear God, seeing thou art in the same condemnation? And we indeed justly; for we receive the due reward of our deeds: but this man hath done nothing amiss. And he said unto Jesus, Lord, remember me when thou comest into thy kingdom. And Jesus said unto him, Verily I say unto thee, Today shalt thou be with me in paradise. And it was about the sixth hour, and there was a darkness over all the earth until the ninth hour. And the sun was darkened, and the veil of the temple was rent in the midst. And when Jesus had cried with a loud voice, he said, Father, into thy hands I commend my spirit: and having said thus, he gave up the ghost. Now when the centurion saw what was done, he glorified God, saying, Certainly this was a righteous man.*

Matthew 27:33-54 KJV *And when they were come unto a place called Golgotha, that is to say, a place of a skull,*

They gave him vinegar to drink mingled with gall: and when he had tasted thereof, he would not drink. And they crucified him, and parted his garments, casting lots: that it might be fulfilled which was spoken by the prophet, They parted my garments among them, and upon my vesture did they cast lots. And sitting down they watched him there; And set up over his head his accusation written, THIS IS JESUS THE KING OF THE JEWS. Then were there two thieves crucified with him, one on the right hand, and another on the left. And they that passed by reviled him, wagging their heads, And saying, Thou that destroyest the temple, and buildest it in three days, save thyself. If thou be the Son of God, come down from the cross. Likewise also the chief priests mocking him, with the scribes and elders, said, He saved others; himself he cannot save. If he be the King of Israel, let him now come down from the cross, and we will believe him. He trusted in God; let him deliver him now, if he will have him: for he said, I am the Son of God. The thieves also, which were crucified with him, cast the same in his teeth. Now from the sixth hour there was darkness over all the land unto the ninth hour. And about the ninth hour Jesus cried with a loud voice, saying, Eli, Eli, lama sabachthani? that is to say, My God, my God, why hast thou forsaken me? Some of them that stood there, when they heard that, said, This man calleth for Elias. And straightway one of them ran, and took a spunge, and filled it with vinegar, and put it on a reed, and gave him to drink. The rest said, Let be, let us see whether Elias will come to save him. Jesus, when he had cried again with a loud voice, yielded up the ghost. And, behold, the veil of the temple was rent in twain from the top to the bottom; and the earth did quake, and the rocks rent; And the graves were opened; and many bodies of the saints which slept arose, And came out of the graves after his resurrection, and went into the holy city, and appeared unto many. Now when the centurion, and they that were with him, watching Jesus, saw the earthquake, and those things that were done, they feared greatly, saying, Truly this was the Son of God.

Jesus was taunted and mocked even while on the cross. Jesus had to bear the painful separation from God the Father, as he bore the sins of the world. Remember Jesus has always been with God the Father, even before coming to earth; and now he has to be completely separated from him. You can tell the way Jesus cries out in the scriptures, "My God, my God, why hast thou forsaken me?" this experience of being separated from God was too much even for him to bear. Although the scriptures doesn't give the exact timing, it does not appear that Jesus desires to live separated from God and gives up the ghost (spirit) and dies. Please take time to really think about that moment that Jesus laid his life down, that it hurt him so much not to be connected to God the Father the way he was accustomed to. Sometimes it is good to slow down, think and meditate on God's word so we can really grasp what has taken place for each one of us.

Another point to mention is that God and pride don't go together. God the Father is in control and has the final say on any and all matters, especially concerning us. God the Father created us, we did not create God the Father knowing this order is essential and critical. Do we understand why God the Father had to kick the enemy out of Heaven? We will review those scriptures as well so it can be a reminder of why humility is required, that God does not tolerate pride.

Isaiah 14:12-16 KJV *How art thou fallen from heaven, O Lucifer, son of the morning! how art thou cut down to the ground, which didst weaken the nations! For thou hast said in thine heart, I will ascend into heaven, I will exalt my throne above the stars of God: I will sit also upon the mount of the congregation, in the sides of the north: I will ascend above the heights of the clouds; I will be like the most High. Yet thou shalt be brought down to hell, to the sides of the pit. They that see thee shall narrowly look upon thee, and consider thee, saying, Is this the man that made the earth to tremble, that did shake kingdoms;*

Ezekiel 28:12-17 NLT *"Son of man, sing this funeral song for the king of Tyre. Give him this message from the Sovereign LORD: "You were the model of perfection, full of wisdom and exquisite in beauty. You were in Eden, the garden of God. Your clothing was adorned with every precious stone- red carnelian, pale-green peridot, white moonstone, blue-green beryl, onyx, green jasper, blue lapis lazuli, turquoise, and emerald-all beautifully crafted for you and set in the finest gold. They were given to you on the day you were created. I ordained and anointed you as the mighty angelic guardian. You had access to the holy mountain of God and walked among the stones of fire. "You were blameless in all you did from the day you were created until the day evil was found in you. Your rich commerce led you to violence, and you sinned. So I banished you in disgrace from the mountain of God. I expelled you, O mighty guardian, from your place among the stones of fire. Your heart was filled with pride because of all your beauty. Your wisdom was corrupted by your love of splendor. So I threw you to the ground and exposed you to the curious gaze of kings.*

As we read these scriptures about the enemy we can see the mistakes that he made. His mistakes in pride were not just in what he said verbally, but also what he thought in his heart. Let this serve as reminder to us that we should be fully aware that God knows us through and through; that he judges not just our words, actions, but our thoughts and our hearts. When we take time to self-reflect that is the time to search our hearts, thoughts, words and actions. The times that we live in self-reflection should occur throughout the day.

The enemy allowed pride to come into his heart and it spread into his actions. It wasn't long before the enemy thought he could overthrow God from his own throne and Kingdom. Imagine that pride unfortunately opened the door to a rebellion and uprising that would change the world for many generations to come. Revelation 12:9 KJV *And the great dragon was cast out, that old serpent, called the Devil, and Satan, which deceiveth the whole world: he was cast out into the earth, and his angels were cast out with him.* How could the creation think it would rule over the Creator? As we go through the last and evil days let us remember to ask ourselves the same question. Why would we challenge God and his Holy Word when he knows what is best for us? Is it possible that we have a pride issue buried deep within our hearts?

If we haven't noticed God the Father is humble and clothed in humility. So, he can require that we too be humble as well. The mere act of making sure that humanity has the gift of salvation through Jesus Christ's sacrifice is one of the great acts of love and humility on display. God the Father loves us all so much that he let his only son die in our places so we could have eternal life when we accept Jesus Christ as the Son of God. Since Jesus and the Father are one, another way of looking at this is Jesus helped make this world, now he has to leave Father God and come to earth and die for it. We have to see that Jesus and Father God are two of the most humble beings, therefore so should we.

There's no way around it we have to humble ourselves while we still have the time. There are benefits to being humble that we will study in the scriptures. (Please note these are not all of the scriptures on humility or being humble.)

Proverbs 15:33 KJV *The fear of the LORD is the instruction of wisdom; and before honour is **humility**.*

Proverbs 18:12 KJV *Before destruction the heart of man is haughty, and before honour is **humility**.*

Proverbs 22:4 KJV *By **humility** and the fear of the LORD are riches, and honour, and life.*

Proverbs 16:19 KJV *Better it is to be of an **humble** spirit with the lowly, than to divide the spoil with the proud.*

Proverbs 29:23 KJV *A man's pride shall bring him low: but honour shall uphold the **humble** in spirit.*

Isaiah 2:11 KJV *The lofty looks of man shall be **humbled**, and the haughtiness of men shall be bowed down, and the LORD alone shall be exalted in that day.*

Isaiah 5:15 KJV *And the mean man shall be brought down, and the mighty man shall be **humbled**, and the eyes of the lofty shall be **humbled**:*

Deuteronomy 8:2 NKJV *And you shall remember that the LORD your God led you all the way these forty years in the wilderness, to **humble** you and test you, to know* *what was in your heart, whether you would keep His commandments or not.*

Deuteronomy 8:3 NKJV *So He* ***humbled*** *you, allowed you to hunger, and fed you with manna which you did not know nor did your fathers know, that He might make you know that man shall not live by bread alone; but man lives by every word that proceeds from the mouth of the LORD.*

2 Chronicles 7:14 NKJV *If my people, which are called by my name, shall* ***humble*** *themselves, and pray, and seek my face, and turn from their wicked ways; then will I hear from heaven, and will forgive their sin, and will heal their land.*

Job 22:29 KJV *When men are cast down, then thou shalt say, There is lifting up; and he shall save the humble person.*

2 Chronicles 12:6-7 NKJV *Whereupon the princes of Israel and the king* ***humbled*** *themselves; and they said, The LORD is righteous. And when the LORD saw that they* ***humbled*** *themselves, the word of the LORD came to Shemaiah, saying, They have* ***humbled*** *themselves; therefore I will not destroy them, but I will grant them some deliverance; and my wrath shall not be poured out upon Jerusalem by the hand of Shishak.*

2 Chronicles 32:26 NKJV *Notwithstanding Hezekiah* ***humbled*** *himself for the pride of his heart, both he and the inhabitants of Jerusalem, so that the wrath of the* L*ORD* *came not upon them in the days of Hezekiah.*
2 Chronicles 34:27 AMP *"Because your heart was gentle and penitent and you* ***humbled*** *yourself before God when you heard His words against this place and its inhabitants, and* ***humbled*** *yourself before Me, and tore your clothes and wept before Me, I also have heard you," declares the* L*ORD.*

Psalm 10:17 NKJV *LORD, You have heard the desire of the* ***humble****; You will prepare their heart; You will cause Your ear to hear,*

Matthew 18:4 KJV *Whosoever therefore shall humble himself as this little child, the same is greatest in the kingdom of heaven.*

Luke 14:11 KJV *For whosoever exalteth himself shall be abased; and he that* ***humbleth*** *himself shall be exalted.*

Luke 18:14 KJV *I tell you, this man went down to his house justified rather than the other: for every one that exalteth himself shall be abased; and he that* ***humbleth*** *himself shall be exalted.*

1 Peter 5:5-6 KJV *Likewise, ye younger, submit yourselves unto the elder. Yea, all of you be subject one to another, and be clothed with* ***humility****: for God resisteth the proud,*

*and giveth grace to the **humble**. **Humble** yourselves therefore under the mighty hand of God, that he may exalt you in due time:*

James 4:6 KJV *But he giveth more grace. Wherefore he saith, God resisteth the proud, but giveth grace unto the **humble**.*

James 4:10 KJV ***Humble** yourselves in the sight of the Lord, and he shall lift you up.*

The scriptures show us consistently that when we are humble that God will exalt us. Dictionary.com defines exalt as, "To raise in rank, honor, power, character, quality, promote, elevate." Bing.com defines exalt as, "To raise to a higher rank or a position of greater power." Or "Make noble in character, dignify." The humility scriptures also show that before God honors a person, he or she humbled oneself. God warns us of our pride and when we are not humble, he will resist us through people, obstacles, etc. If we refuse to humble ourselves the scriptures warn us that God will humble us, we will be brought down if we don't humble ourselves when we should. The scriptures inform us that God saves or spares the humble punishment that they actually deserve; helps them in times of trouble. God tests us to see where we are spiritually in our hearts and thoughts, will we keep (obey) his commands in tough times, will we choose to humble ourselves. The scriptures show that God wants to forgive us and heal us and humility especially in repentance helps to bring those benefits forth.

An example that makes it easier to see is this, a child that is spoiled rotten overall most people don't want to be bother for too long, and even the parents of that child will have sincere regrets of not raising that child properly. The spoiled child will often talk disrespectfully to his or her parents and to others. The spoiled child will often have a great deal of entitlement and demand to have more than they actually deserve. The spoiled child will often believe that he or she is far better than others, therefore can treat others in any manner. The spoiled child can even become verbally and physically abusive when he or she does not get his or her way. The spoiled child gains a reputation as such, and people don't like to see that child coming their way. The spoiled child brings a great deal of embarrassment and humiliation to his or her parents.

See as we look at the spoiled child can we see things more from God's perspective. He created us, not we ourselves; therefore we must have a proper perspective of who we are and who we actually belong too. A child does not have the right or authority to boss his or her parent around. When we see this happen in real life, usually it bothers us; so why is it okay for us to think we don't have to humble ourselves before God? We do not get to boss God around; we have to be mindful on how we approach God and each other. Since we are God's children he does not want us treating each other arrogantly or pridefully. Even our earthly parents did not like us fighting with or mistreating our siblings, relatives, friends or neighbors; it's the same with God we must treat each other with the love, respect and humility that God desires of us.

Also, as I researched it is clear that humility is an important topic in the Bible because there are well over 100 scriptures that either have the word humility, humble, humbly, etc. or deal with the concept of humility, being or walking humbly. With humility and the concept of humility being mentioned that many times we as believers cannot deny the significance and the importance that it means for us to be humble, especially before God the Father. Remember God's word the Bible (Basic Instructions Before Leave Earth) is true, and that we live off of every word that proceeds out the mouth of God. Matthew 4:4 KJV *But he answered and said, It is written, Man shall not live by bread alone, but by every word that proceedeth out of the mouth of God.* God's word on humility will help us to avoid a great deal of unnecessary problems and stressful situations. God's word on humility will help us to live the life that he is calling us to live, our humility opens the door for God to take our ordinary and make us supernaturally extraordinary. The other saying that the saints of old would say, "God can only use us so much when you are full of pride." Let's remember that when we are puffed up or filled with pride, that we open the door for the enemy to bring attacks against us and that even God will resist us. That's not the place that we want to be, humility is one of the keys to doing great things for GOD ALMIGHTY!

We have to remember that we are not here to stay, at some point we will transition and no longer be in the land of the living. The reality check that when we die, this world keeps on going and although our loved ones grieve the loss of us, they will go on. The saying there is life after death, and life goes on is true. Therefore we should think with the end in mind and know that we won't always be here. When we truly humble ourselves it makes it easier to understand that God is in control and can utilize whom he pleases. That it's not all about one person, no matter how greatly God uses that person to accomplish his will.

Chapter 3 Summary

Why Should We Demonstrate Humility?

- **Jesus Christ was humble, we are his followers we too will be humble.**

- **Philippians 2:8 KJV *And being found in fashion as a man, he humbled himself, and became obedient unto death, even the death of the cross.***

- **Jesus endured too much before going to the crucifixation and during the crucifixation for anyone to refuse to humble oneself.**

- **Jesus endured the painful separation from God the Father, to bear the whole world's sins; as hard as it was for him.**

- **The enemy was kicked out of Heaven for his pride and rebellion against God.**

- **The mere acts of God the Father and Jesus Christ the Son of God are clothed in humility, the salvation plan; Jesus died for a world that rightfully belonged to him.**

- **God searches our words, actions, thoughts and hearts; there is no fooling God about anything,** especially when it comes to pride and a refusal to walk in humility.

- There are benefits to humility:
    - God will bless us with honor, promote us and increase our character and stature (rank) in him.
    - God desires to spare us being resisted by him, people and situations.
    - God desires not to punish us.
    - God will save us in times of trouble.
    - God sees that we keep his commandments in hard times and repent of our sins.
    - God will forgive, heal and restore us. (He won't withhold any good thing from us, as we walk uprightly before him. Psalm 84:11)

- When we refuse to humble ourselves we are bringing embarrassment not just to ourselves, but to those around us, AND to God the Father.

- There are well over 100 scriptures on humility and the concept of humility, therefore HUMILITY is not only required but IMPORTANT.

- Since we don't live off mere bread alone but off of every word that proceeds out the mouth of God, then

we know the scriptures on humility must be our way of life.

- **God's word on humility will help us to live the life that he is calling us to live, our humility opens the door for God to take our ordinary and make us supernaturally extraordinary.**

- **Puffed up with PRIDE is not the place that we want to be, humility is one of the keys to doing great things for GOD ALMIGHTY!**

- **We won't always be in the land of the living, the world keeps going when we transition to eternal life.**

Chapter 4
How Do We Show Humility?

We show humility by making the conscious choice each day, moment, decision by doing what is right and believing and being in agreement that God's word is true, especially the scriptures on humility. When we interact with others we do so with a heart of humility, esteeming them higher than we esteem ourselves. That means we consciously promote others; their well-being and accomplishments and we do not promote ourselves. We can share what we are doing but it should not be in an excessive manner that when people encounter us we are consistently talking about ourselves and what we have achieved until people get tired of us.

Studying God's word is a very important part of the humility process. 2 Timothy 2:15 KJV states, *"Study to shew thyself approved unto God, a workman that needeth not to be ashamed, rightly dividing the word of truth."* Overall humility doesn't come easily, so we have to do our part and make sure we are studying, memorizing and meditating on the humility scriptures on a daily basis. When we make an effort to study his word and ask God in prayer how to apply the word effectively, God is faithful to answer that prayer.

Another way we show humility is by obeying God's words concerning humility. As we study, memorize, and meditate on the scriptures it should help us to actually do what the scriptures are telling us to do. It's not enough to know the scriptures but we have to do what God says. It will take discipline, and the times we live in now supernatural discipline to consistently obey God's word each day of our lives.

Remember Moses example of humility he was fully aware of his limitations, and was always humble enough to ask God for help. Knowing ourselves the good and the bad, our strengths and our weaknesses and demonstrating humility in asking God for help is invaluable. Remember Jesus mentioned we needed to be like a child; friendly reminder children are totally dependent on their parents. As God's children we have to be totally dependent on God the Father, when we are not that's usually when we find ourselves in situations that are just too much for us; and then we have to cry out that God save us from those situations and from ourselves.

We show humility through a consistent prayer life with God the Father. As we show God we are totally dependent on him, we must pray on a daily basis about being humble. That we show God on a consistent basis that we do not want pride to consume us or destroy us; that we truly desire from our heart to be humble before

God the Father and others. This should be a daily prayer for us because the enemy knows how to tempt us to be arrogant or prideful. The society or world that we live in sends a lot of messages that it's okay to be pompous and that's not true at all. God's word has the final say on how we should conduct ourselves. Remember God's Word is usually in direct opposition of the world's view, standards, norms and customs.

We show humility through a surrendered heart that wants to give God the glory day in and day out. We don't want to fall into a false humility that is for show before others, because God knows our inner thoughts and our hearts too. God knows whether we are really being humble sincerely or not. The sooner we are able to accept that God knows our motives, thoughts and what is prompting our actions, decisions and conversations, the easier it will be for us. It's better to come clean with God about who we really are, and as we journey on this faith walk, God will reveal where we really are in him. Sometimes we are much further along than we give ourselves credit for and other times we have given ourselves too much credit and have a long way to go. What God reveals to us about ourselves is a very humbling experience.

Embracing that we are truly sinners saved by grace is how we demonstrate humility before God and others. Romans

3:23 KJV *For all have sinned, and come short of the glory of God.* As we grow in knowledge and wisdom of God we have to be careful that we do not allow what we have learned about God and the things of God to puff us up. Let's look at 1 Corinthians 8:1 in different translations to gain a fuller picture and a much better understanding.

1 Corinthians 8:1 KJV *Now as touching things offered unto idols, we know that we all have knowledge. Knowledge puffeth up, but charity edifieth.*

1 Corinthians 8:1 AMP *Now about food sacrificed to idols, we know that we all have knowledge [concerning this]. Knowledge [alone] makes [people self-righteously] arrogant, but love [that unselfishly seeks the best for others] builds up and encourages others to grow [in wisdom].*

1 Corinthians 8:1 AMPC *Now about food offered to idols: of course we know that all of us possess knowledge [concerning these matters. Yet mere] knowledge causes people to be puffed up (to bear themselves loftily and be proud), but love (affection and goodwill and benevolence) edifies and builds up and encourages one to grow [to his full stature].*

1 Corinthians 8:1 GNT *Now, concerning what you wrote about food offered to idols. It is true, of course, that "all of*

us have knowledge," as they say. Such knowledge, however, puffs a person up with pride; but love builds up.

God's word is very clear that as we gain knowledge we can use it the wrong way. To avoid this trap we should be consistently praying that as God elevates us in knowledge and stature with him and others that we choose to remain humble. That we don't want to let God down in this area, especially in the times that we live in. We should be asking God to help us to see things through his perspective and not our own, others or the world's perspectives. When we get out of the trap of BIG "I" and little you, knowing that God loves us all and that our titles, successes, works and deeds do not give us license to look down on others. That we don't use our promotions and elevations in God to judge and condemn others either. The trap of self-righteousness can be a very dangerous one, and it is the wisdom of God to avoid it as much as possible.

Heavenly Father we come before you with a desire to be more humble. Would you help us to surrender to you on a daily basis as we study, memorize, meditate and pray your Holy Word? Would you soften our hearts where they are hardened? As we learn to desire to please you in every area of our lives thank you for blessing us with hearts that truly want to be humble and that allow us to walk in humility on a consistent basis. Lord as you bless, promote and elevate us thank you that we will be more vigilant to consciously choose to

remain humble. That we will consistently give you the GLORY, PRASIE AND CREDIT for all that you are doing in our lives. Lord would you help us to remember to esteem others more than ourselves by speaking highly of and promoting them, whenever possible. Please help us not to judge or condemn others, we understand that is your arena not ours. Father God as you reveal our strengths, weaknesses and limitations thank you for helping us to pray about them on a consistent basis, that we desire to glorify you in Jesus Mighty Name Amen and Amen.

Chapter 4 Summary

How Do We Show Humility?

- **Through a daily conscious choice.**

- **Studying, memorizing and meditating on God's word on a daily basis.**

- **Obeying (actually doing what) God's word says about humility.**

- **Knowing our own limitations; knowing our strengths and weaknesses. Being dependent on God the Father for help.**

- **Through a consistent prayer life.**

- **From a surrendered heart that desires to be humble before God the Father and others.**

- **Embracing that we are truly sinners saved by grace. Romans 3:23 KJV**

- **Refusing to let our knowledge to cause us to be full of pride, arrogance and self-righteousness.**

Chapter 5

When Do You Show Humility?

Humility should be shown in just about every situation you can think of. Let's think of the times when we saw a great deal of pride, arrogance and pompousness. Do we remember the impact that much pride had on that situation and the people involved in it? Did the pride that we saw help the situation or did it make matters worse? Were the people aware of their pride and how it was impacting others? Was the situation harder to watch and endure because those involved were full of pride to the point that they were blinded by it? It's good to reflect on people and situations where we have not seen humility, it will help us to be more aware when we are ourselves are not being humble.

Now we will ask the more important questions of ourselves. Do we remember times when we were prideful? How did people respond to us? What did it cost us? If we had another chance what things would we do differently? The reality is we don't have the power to control or change others, or change the past. But we do have the power to work on ourselves and allow God to transform us into who he is calling us to be through a consistent prayer life, studying, memorizing and meditating, and living out his Holy Word.

For example most people usually don't want to be last, our corrupted flesh has a way of putting us first no matter the situation. As we grow in God it should become easier to be okay with not always being the first person to accomplish certain things, etc.

When you have disagreements have you matured to the point:

That you don't have to raise your voice to get your point across?

That you don't have to have the final word or say on the matter?

That you can admit when you are wrong?

That you may not have all the facts to make the best decisions?

That you realize what's really at stake if this is not handled with love?

When you become angry have you matured to the point:

That you don't have to lash out at others or take your problems out on others?

That you don't become negative through gossiping, backbiting, complaining and murmuring?

That you don't have to tell everyone what has happened?

When things aren't going your way have you matured to the point:

That you still do what God asks of you?

That you still pray, fast, study, memorize, meditate and live out God's Holy Word?

That you still trust God in spite of the trials, tribulations and persecutions that you face?

That you still love God and others as you are commanded to do?

That you still bless and help others, even when you need help yourself?

When you are right have you matured to the point:

That you no longer have to argue until you feel you have won?

That you keep a respectful tone when talking to others?

That others may refuse to see that you are right and that you don't feel compelled to persuade them to see it your way?

When God promotes and elevates you, have you matured to the point:

That the high standard that God holds you to, you don't try to enforce that on everyone else?

That you do not abuse your God given authority and power over others?

That you can accept as God's leader you make mistakes and even hurt others whether intentionally or unintentionally?

That as God's leader you still know how to esteem others higher than yourself? (Encourage, speak highly of others, promote others more than yourself?)

That you show appreciation for what others do?

That you correct others in love?

When God's leaders make mistakes, have you matured to the point:

That you know to pray and intercede for them right away?

That you can still respect and submit to their authority?

That you can handle what they have done without telling everyone about it?

That you aren't quick to be in their face for every mistake they make?

These are just some questions to get you thinking about how you handle different situations on any given day. The answers you give to the questions will reveal where you currently are in your level of spiritual maturity and **humility**. Also, it will show areas of improvement that you can take to God in prayer and commit to studying the scriptures to help with those areas.

Chapter 5 Summary

When Do We Show Humility?

- **RIGHT NOW.**

- **In every situation, humility is required.**

- **Remember the times in our lives when pride made matters worse.**

- **Life has many challenges, obstacles that we all must face, but how we handle them reveals not only our level of spiritual maturity, but our level of humility as well.**

Chapter 6

Where Do We Show Humility?

Humility should be demonstrated everywhere. Sometimes we can be guilty of being humble at church, but then at home there is a huge difference on how we interact at home. Humility is required of us everywhere we go. The thought of being humble in just certain places has to be replaced with a much better thought that we are to be humble everywhere we go.

If we really understood how Biblical principles should start at home and proceed from there it would make a huge difference in our lives. Overall at some point in our lives we usually spend more time at home, so it is a good idea to practice humility there so it easier to demonstrate it to others outside our home. When our loved ones at home can see us working to humble ourselves in our interactions with them, it will make a difference in their lives and in the household as a whole.

When our families can sincerely vouch for us that we live the life that we talk about, that is far more impactful. For too long some have thought that because we are God's leaders or servants that some of God's commands and instructions don't apply to us. However, that is very far from the truth, the enemy can trick and deceive even the best of us. Yet, it does not have to be that way, especially when we understand as Believers of Christ we are called to uphold a Godly standard before God the Father and people too, and especially before our families.

What would our families say about our humility or lack thereof? How many examples of humility or pride would they be able to share about us? Would we be motivated to do better based on what they would say? Or would it be encouragement to keep going because in some areas we are on the right track?

When our family members do something we don't like, do we have to tell the whole world about it? Have we learned how to take our problems directly to those relatives that we have an issue or disagreement with? Have we made a commitment in our hearts to truly reconcile with our relatives, that we won't allow petty or major disagreements to come between one another? That we value the family and will not allow the enemy to get a foothold to sow discord and division.

Practicing humility allows one to see the much bigger picture. There is more to life and our interactions with people then just right and wrong. I like the way a man of God said, "I could be right and be all alone." See he understood being humble meant he would not be alone, that he would still have his family. Sometimes as people we need time to really be able to see ourselves, so it does not always help that we demand that our loved ones see it our way. Let's face it there are few perspectives to keep in mind but ultimately there is one that always wins out. There's your perspective, others perspective and GOD's perspective. Of course GOD's perspective wins out! Yet it takes people clothed in humility to know that God's perspective and way is the best way.

Do we show humility when we are out in public places? Sometimes when we are out in public that's where you can see that humility is really lacking. Could I encourage us to be the difference maker when we are out and about in public? That we treat the store clerk, fast food cashier, postal clerk, city worker, etc. with dignity and respect on a consistent basis, even when they are not courteous with us. Let's resist the temptation to go off, tell someone off or cuss them out because they get our order wrong or disrespect us in some way. Can we pass the test of showing humility in public even when we have been disrespected?

When we are driving in the car, can we show humility there? When we hear the stories about road rage, we definitely don't want to be a part of that. Can we be committed to driving with humility even with the chaotic driving that is going on around us? Let's resist the temptation to cut someone off because they cut us off.

Instead of forcing our way into a lane, let's demonstrate patience and get in the lane when it is safe to do so.

Funerals and memorials are good place to demonstrate humility. When they ask us to be respectful and honor the family's request to keep remarks to two to five minutes, are we able to do that? If not, it's time for humility to come in. Everyone can't get up and speak at the funeral or memorial service. Also, the funeral director has to get the body to the cemetery by a certain time. If a funeral or memorial service is planned for one hour, it should not end up being two to four hours long because everyone wanted to speak and the eulogy was too long. It takes humility to realize that the funeral director has a plan and other duties besides our loved ones funeral or memorial services.

Our workplace is another place that humility should be shown by us. With all of the office politics and cutthroat tactics that go on in any given day, especially in Corporate America; Believers in Christ this is the time to show God and our co-workers what Godly humility looks like. Do we do our best to avoid the conversations on gossiping, backbiting, and slandering others? When someone is bullying or ganging up on someone, do we intervene in a way that is loving and humble; or do we come across self-righteously? When others are pushing and clamoring for the promotion and doing whatever it takes, are we able to maintain our dignity, respect and humility and let our work ethic shine forth?

Business owners are you able to maintain a quality work environment? Or do you run your business in a way that comes across more like a dictatorship? How do you handle those that disagree with you? Do you embarrass them and put them on the spot? Do you have a territorial spirit about yourself, that says this is my business and if you don't like that get out? We have to be careful how we conduct and run our businesses? It may be our business but God is still in charge we have to remember that. Do our workers fear us instead of respecting us? Would our workers say we are humble? It's hard to run a business that glorifies God without humility.

Our ministry or church is where humility should be shown by us. We have to be careful that as God elevates and promotes us that we are not abusing our authority over others. We have to remember God's way is in direct opposition to the world's way. When we see the gifts that others have can we remain humble and not be intimidated to the point that we go to the leaders and report concerns that really don't exist? Humility will help us avoid petty competition, we are not to be competing with each other, but helping each other and working as team. Humility helps us to keep the goals in mind on why God has called us to ministry or to a certain church.

Social media is another place that we should demonstrate humility. Unfortunately, social media has become more and more of a giant in the last decade or so. We can find just about anything on social media and there is a lot of hatred, racism, oppression, bullying and pride just to name a few! Can God count on us to demonstrate love, kindness and humility on social media? When we help others can we use humility on what we post?

Instead of posting pictures of people getting water and other necessities, could we just post the gifts, water, food, etc. without the people being in the photos? Or at least be sure to ask permission from the people who are in need before taking their photos and posting on social media. Humility and wisdom gives another perspective that when people are at one of the lowest points in their life, it is not right to exploit them as they go through a very difficult time.

When others are posting things that are hateful, divisive, etc., can God count on us to post things that glorify him: encouragement, kindness, good deeds, etc.? A humble heart remembers once we become Believers in Christ that we are in this world, but no longer of this world. That means we live in this world, but we are working very hard not to operate like this world. Are we posting things that encourage us to be humble? Are we more concerned about getting a lot of likes rather than standing for God?

Let me encourage you to be the difference maker on social media, that posting uplifting posts, scriptures, prayers, salvation prayer, good deeds, etc. is a way of glorifying God with your social media accounts.

My prayer is that these questions will get us thinking about the various places we can demonstrate humility. Ultimately as we grow spiritually we should be more aware of ways to really glorify God. Remember faith without works is dead; James 4:26 KJV *For as the body without the spirit is dead, so faith without works is dead also.* When we show our faith through love and humble actions God will get the glory, especially when we as Believers are quick to give God the praise. Matthew 5:16 KJV *Let your light so shine before men, that they may see your good works, and glorify your Father which is in heaven.* There are scriptures like these that should help us to focus on what's really important as we go about living a life that really glorifies God the Father.

Heavenly Father would you please help us to remember that we are to demonstrate love and humility wherever we go? Could you help us to remember to live out Matthew 5:16 to the best of our ability, each day of our lives? Lord we have hearts that want to glorify you and we understand that it's hard to do that without humility. Lord thank you for helping us to become more aware that you are everywhere and you see all that we do. Father God could you please give us the strength to

resist the temptation not to humble ourselves? Lord thank you for clothing us in humility in our words, deeds, and lifestyle too as we set out to demonstrate humility everywhere we go in Jesus Might Name Amen and Amen.

Chapter 6 Summary

Where Do We Show Humility?

- **EVERYWHERE!**

- **As believers we must start and practice HUMILITY AT HOME FIRST.**

- **God see us everywhere we go, there's no hiding if we are demonstrating humility or not.**

- **Remember we are in this world, but not of this world. We live in this world, but we are striving to live for God, not like the world.**

- **As we demonstrate our faith through love and humility we are living out Matthew 5:16 KJV *Let your light so shine before men, that they may see your good works, and glorify your Father which is in heaven.***

Chapter 7

Summary & Salvation Prayer

Thank you for going on this journey to a better understanding that Humility is Required. When we see things the way God sees them then we are headed in the right direction. PRIDE is a serious offense before God; therefore we must take the humility process and journey seriously. The following expressions are reminders that Humility is Required:

The way up in the Kingdom of God is down.

What goes up, must come down. (Pride comes before the fall.)

Do you want God to humble you or do you choose to humble yourself?

God can only use you so much when you are full of pride.

Remember when the disciples argued who would be the greatest amongst them, Jesus made sure they knew their focus was way off. That his Kingdom did not operate like the world did. The world lords their positions and power over people, like a dictator would because that's their view of greatness; yet Jesus says in the Kingdom of God that the people who choose to humble themselves and serve others are the greatest. We have to remember that Jesus's teachings and God's Holy Word is in direct opposition to this world's ways and views.

Humility is required of everyone; we all have to humble ourselves before Almighty God. God and pride do not go together at all, they do not mix. The offense of the enemy's pride and rebellion was so serious that he and some angels were kicked out of Heaven. Hell was created for the adversary and the third of the angels, it was never intended for humanity. Matthew 25:41 GNT *"Then he will say to those on his left, 'Away from me, you that are under God's curse! Away to the eternal fire which has been prepared for the Devil and his angels!*

Remember we are in this world, but not of this world; we don't or shouldn't operate like the world does, we must operate like God says we should and what Jesus showed us in his actions and teachings. God desires the best for us and he knows the plan that is perfect for us, when we humble ourselves we can achieve that perfected plan that God has for our lives. Pride has a way of really blinding us, that's why it is so important that we choose to humble ourselves. The enemy knows he can take us off track with pride, the times that we are living in we do not want to miss God now! If ever there was a time to stay close to God as possible now is that time, we do not want pride, arrogance, or self-righteousness separating us from God, we do not want God resisting us in these last and evil days.

Even those who use a more common vernacular are familiar with the sayings, "The sun does not rise and set on just you." and "The world does not evolve around you." Truth be told they are not just sayings they are the truth; we will not live forever in this lifetime. When we have a humble perspective we realize that one day we will pass away, yet this Earth will keep on spinning, keep on going without us. So, whenever we begin to think to highly of ourselves or what we do is so great, the reminder that we won't always be here helps us to balance out and truly humble ourselves before God and people too.

God has given us great examples in the Bible of people who were humble and those who were prideful. Let's take time to study their examples as often as possible so we can learn from their obedience and their disobedience. When we study God's word it is always a good idea to have a notebook to write notes or even have a Bible that we can write in and highlight scriptures that stand out or speak to us. It takes work through studying, memorizing, meditating, hearing, praying and living God's word to crucify this flesh; but remember:

Uncrucified Flesh = PRIDE and Crucified Flesh = Humility.

Remember It's Praying Time and HUMILITY IS REQUIRED! God has long suffered with us for quite some time now, we can no longer go about things in our own way, it's God's way now. God requires us to be humble, it's time to accept and submit to that while there is still time.

Below are some humility and pride scriptures that will be useful to pray, meditate, memorize and live as one walks on this humility journey.

Humility & Pride Scriptures

Romans 12:3 KJV *For I say, through the grace given unto me, to every man that is among you, not to think of himself more highly than he ought to think; but to think soberly, according as God hath dealt to every man the measure of faith.*

Philippians 2:3-4 NLT *Don't be selfish; don't try to impress others. Be humble, thinking of others as better than yourselves. Don't look out only for your own interests, but take an interest in others, too.*

Proverbs 16:18-19 KJV *Pride goeth before destruction, and an haughty spirit before a fall. Better it is to be of an humble spirit with the lowly, than to divide the spoil with the proud.*

Proverbs 25:6 NLT *Don't demand an audience with the king or push for a place among the great.*

Mark 9:33-37 NLT *After they arrived at Capernaum and settled in a house, Jesus asked his disciples, "What were you discussing out on the road?" But they didn't answer, because they had been arguing about which of them was the greatest. He sat down, called the twelve disciples over to him, and said, "Whoever wants to be first must take last place and be the servant of everyone else." Then he put a little child among them. Taking the child in his arms, he said to them, "Anyone who welcomes a little child like this on my behalf welcomes me, and anyone who welcomes me welcomes not only me but also my Father who sent me."*

Luke 18:10-14 KJV *Two men went up into the temple to pray; the one a Pharisee, and the other a publican. The Pharisee stood and prayed thus with himself, God, I thank thee, that I am not as other men are, extortioners, unjust, adulterers, or even as this publican. I fast twice in the week, I give tithes of all that I possess. And the publican, standing afar off, would not lift up so much as his eyes unto heaven, but smote upon his breast, saying, God be merciful to me a sinner. I tell you, this man went down to his house justified rather than the other: for every one that exalteth himself shall be abased; and he that humbleth himself shall be exalted.*

Psalm 25:8-9 GNT *Because the LORD is righteous and good, he teaches sinners the path they should follow. He leads the humble in the right way and teaches them his will.*

Ephesians 4:1-3 KJV *I therefore, the prisoner of the Lord, beseech you that ye walk worthy of the vocation wherewith ye are called, With all lowliness and meekness, with longsuffering, forbearing one another in love; Endeavouring to keep the unity of the Spirit in the bond of peace.*

Ephesians 4:1-3 NLT *Therefore I, a prisoner for serving the Lord, beg you to lead a life worthy of your calling, for you have been called by God. Always be humble and gentle. Be patient with each other, making allowance for each other's faults because of your love. Make every effort to keep yourselves united in the Spirit, binding yourselves together with peace.*

Daniel 4:37 KJV *Now I Nebuchadnezzar praise and extol and honour the King of heaven, all whose works are truth, and his ways judgment: and those that walk in pride he is able to abase.*

2 Samuel 22:28 GNT *You save those who are humble, but you humble those who are proud.*

Matthew 6:1-4 NLT *"Watch out! Don't do your good deeds publicly, to be admired by others, for you will lose the reward from your Father in heaven. When you give to someone in need, don't do as the hypocrites do—blowing trumpets in the synagogues and streets to call attention to their acts of charity! I tell you the truth, they have received all the reward they will ever get. But when you give to someone in need, don't let your left hand know what your right hand is doing. Give your gifts in private, and your Father, who sees everything, will reward you.*

1 Corinthians 15:9 NLT *For I am the least of all the apostles. In fact, I'm not even worthy to be called an apostle after the way I persecuted God's church.*

Philippians 2:8 KJV *And being found in fashion as a man, he humbled himself, and became obedient unto death, even the death of the cross.*

Psalm 18:27 NLT *You rescue the humble, but you humiliate the proud.*

Zechariah 9:9 AMP *Rejoice greatly, O Daughter of Zion! Shout aloud, O Daughter of Jerusalem! Behold, your King (Messianic King) is coming to you; He is righteous and endowed with salvation, Humble and unassuming [in submission to the will of the Father] and riding on a donkey, Upon a colt, the foal of a donkey.*

Luke 1:51-52 AMP *"He has done mighty deeds with His [powerful] arm; He has scattered those who were proud in the thoughts of their heart. "He has brought down rulers from their thrones, And exalted those who were humble.*

Luke 10:45 AMP *For even the Son of Man did not come to be served, but to serve, and to give His life as a ransom for many."*

Matthew 18:4 AMP *Therefore, whoever humbles himself like this child is greatest in the kingdom of heaven.*

2 Chronicles 34:27 AMP *"Because your heart was gentle and penitent and you humbled yourself before God when you heard His words against this place and its inhabitants, and humbled yourself before Me, and tore your clothes and wept before Me, I also have heard you," declares the LORD.*

Proverbs 27:2 NLT *Let someone else praise you, not your own mouth—a stranger, not your own lips.*

Deuteronomy 8:2-3 AMPC *And you shall [earnestly] remember all the way which the Lord your God led you these forty years in the wilderness, to humble you and to prove you, to know what was in your [mind and] heart, whether you would keep His commandments or not. And He humbled you and allowed you to hunger and fed you with manna, which you did not know nor did your fathers know, that He might make you recognize and personally know that man does not live by bread only, but man lives by every word that proceeds out of the mouth of the Lord.*

Psalm 147:6 AMP *The LORD lifts up the humble; He casts the wicked down to the ground.*

Zephaniah 2:3 GNT *Turn to the LORD, all you humble people of the land, who obey his commands. Do what is right, and humble yourselves before the LORD. Perhaps you will escape punishment on the day when the LORD shows his anger.*

Psalm 101:5 NKJV *Whoever secretly slanders his neighbor, Him I will destroy; The one who has a haughty look and a proud heart, Him I will not endure.*

Psalm 18:27 NLT *You rescue the humble, but you humiliate the proud.*

Proverbs 16:5 KJV *Every one that is proud in heart is an abomination to the LORD: though hand join in hand, he shall not be unpunished.*

Proverbs 16:5 AMP *Everyone who is proud and arrogant in heart is disgusting and exceedingly offensive to the LORD; Be assured he will not go unpunished.*

Heavenly Father we approach your throne with a Holy boldness but with a gracious humility. We come seeking you to ask for your continual guidance and help on this humility journey. We ask that you would send loving reminders when we begin to puff up with pride. Father God could you help us to fully embrace that not only is it praying time, but HUMILITY IS REQUIRED of all of us.

Would you help us to study the humility and pride scriptures, so we can see the benefits, warnings and consequences? God would you give us a SUPERNATURAL INCREASE IN SPIRITUAL MATURITY AND DISCERNMENT to see things the way that you see them? Please forgive us for not seeing pride as the sin it really is. Help us to draw closer to you than ever before and would you please help us not to resist the seasons of consecration and lowliness? Could you give us a heart that desires to partner with your plans and processes for our lives? Could you give us a heart that desires to walk in humility on a daily basis? Lord when we pray sincerely and humbly we know that you hear our prayers in Jesus Mighty Name Amen and Amen.

We want to make the most of every opportunity to win souls for Jesus Christ. The truth is eternity is closer for some than others. We are not just living for this life, but we are surely living for the life to come. Let me encourage you do not delay in saying this Salvation Prayer. Please repeat this prayer from a sincere heart.

Dear Lord Jesus, I know that I am a sinner, and I ask you for your forgiveness. I believe you died for my sins and rose from the dead. I turn from my sins, and invite You to come into my heart and life. I ask for the Holy Spirit to dwell in me, to guide me, and to teach me all things. I choose to trust and follow You as the Son of God and LORD and Savior in Jesus name Amen and Amen.

If you repeated that prayer with a true sincerity you JUST GOT SAVED!!! We encourage you to read your Bible on a daily basis. Here are your next steps:

1) **Download the free Bible App https://www.youversion.com/the-bible-app/.**
2) **Get a paper Parallel Study Bible that has King James Version(KJV) and another version of your choice that helps you to understand the scriptures better.**
3) **Read the Bible every day.**
4) **Ask God the Father to lead you to a church home where the Bible is taught and preached in a way that you can understand it and live it out daily.**

Lastly if you repeated the Salvation Prayer and got saved please email us at itsprayingtime2020@gmail.com, we would like to pray for you and encourage you along your spiritual journey. You can also email us your prayer requests and we would be glad to stand in the gap for you.

Author's Biography

Dr. Kimberly K. Clayton is making a conscious choice to humble herself on a daily basis. She is currently working on another biblical project with goals to represent Jesus Christ to the fullest, win as many souls for Jesus Christ as possible, recruit and train additional godly intercessors, and to continue to pray and intercede as God has called her to do. She lives with her daughter, Elise, who is her pride and joy!

She is the founder and leader of "It's Praying Time," a ministry where prayer intercession and training takes place on a weekly basis. Dr. Kimberly believes in the power of prayer and intercession and is determined to help others grow in this calling through the prayer line, Facebook Live and YouTube. You are welcome to become a subscriber to our "It's Praying Time" You Tube Channel. "It's Praying Time" is focused on reaching as many people as possible for Jesus Christ through various means and platforms.

Dr. Kimberly Clayton is also an ordained and licensed minister through the "School of the Prophet" which is led by their fearless leader, Prophetess Renee Gordon. One of Kimberly's most prized moments is when she and her young daughter, Elise, had their second baptism together through the "School of the Prophet". She also treasures being able to serve on other prayer lines when needed.

www.ingramcontent.com/pod-product-compliance
Lightning Source LLC
LaVergne TN
LVHW020648100826
845148LV00012B/2377